TOOLS FOR CAREGIVERS

- **F&P LEVEL:** B
- **WORD COUNT:** 28
- **CURRICULUM CONNECTIONS:** mammals, colors, patterns, textures

Skills to Teach

- **HIGH-FREQUENCY WORDS:** I, see
- **CONTENT WORDS:** dark, fluffy, fur, light, long, spotted, striped
- **PUNCTUATION:** exclamation point, periods
- **WORD STUDY:** long /e/, spelled ee (*see*); long /e/, spelled y (*fluffy*); long /i/, spelled igh (*light*)
- **TEXT TYPE:** information report

Before Reading Activities

- Read the title and give a simple statement of the main idea.
- Have students "walk" through the book and talk about what they see in the pictures.
- Introduce new vocabulary by having students predict the first letter and locate the word in the text.
- Discuss any unfamiliar concepts that are in the text.

After Reading Activities

Explain to readers that mammals have fur. It helps keep the animals warm. Do readers recognize any of the mammals in the book? Show them more examples. Can they name others? Write their answers on the board. Then, show pictures of each mammal they listed. Ask readers to describe the fur of each.

Tadpole Books are published by Jump!, 5357 Penn Avenue South, Minneapolis, MN 55419, www.jumplibrary.com

Copyright ©2023 Jump!. International copyright reserved in all countries. No part of this book may be reproduced in any form without written permission from the publisher.

Editor: Jenna Gleisner **Designer:** Molly Ballanger

Photo Credits: Ian 2010/Shutterstock, cover; Eric Isselee/Shutterstock, 1, 2bl, 8–9; David Osborn/Shutterstock, 2tl, 4–5; Dnaveh/Dreamstime, 2tr, 14–15; Pharo/Shutterstock, 2ml, 3; meunierd/Shutterstock, 2mr, 6–7; Rudi Hulshof/Shutterstock, 2br, 10–11; Natalia Fedosova/Shutterstock, 12–13; Shutterstock, 16.

Library of Congress Cataloging-in-Publication Data
Names: Gleisner, Jenna Lee, author.
Title: Fur / by Jenna Lee Gleisner.
Description: Minneapolis, MN: Jump!, Inc., (2023)
Series: I see animal textures! | Includes index.
Audience: Ages 3–6
Identifiers: LCCN 2022011516 (print)
LCCN 2022011517 (ebook)
ISBN 9798885240413 (hardcover)
ISBN 9798885240420 (paperback)
ISBN 9798885240437 (ebook)
Subjects: LCSH: Fur—Juvenile literature.
Classification: LCC QL942 .G635 2023 (print) | LCC QL942 (ebook) | DDC 599.7147—dc23/eng/20220317
LC record available at https://lccn.loc.gov/2022011516
LC ebook record available at https://lccn.loc.gov/2022011517

I SEE ANIMAL TEXTURES!
FUR

by Jenna Lee Gleisner

TABLE OF CONTENTS

Words to Know 2

Fur 3

Let's Review! 16

Index 16

WORDS TO KNOW

dark

fluffy

fur

light

spotted

striped

FUR

fur

I see fur.

I see dark fur.

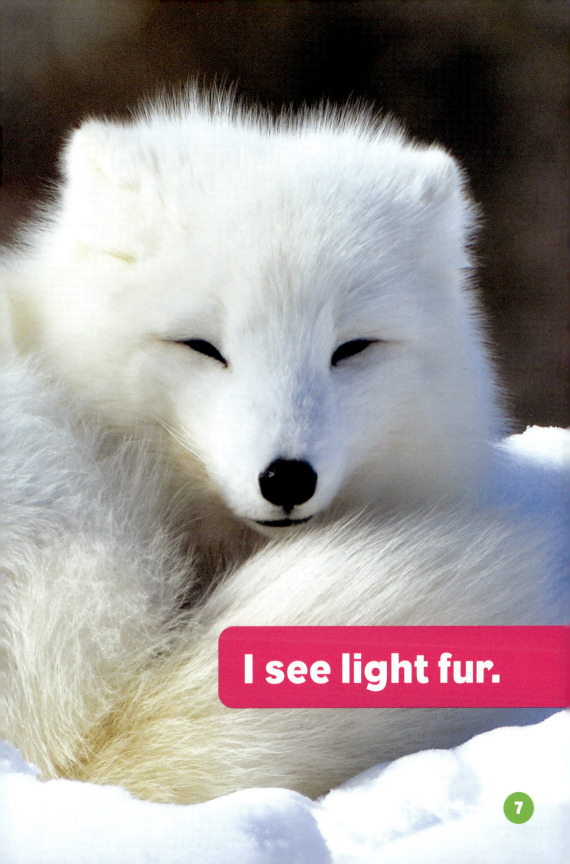

I see light fur.

I see spotted fur.

stripe

I see striped fur.

I see long fur.

I see fluffy fur!

LET'S REVIEW!

Mammals have fur. Fur keeps animals safe and warm. What kinds of fur do you see below?

INDEX

dark 5

fluffy 15

light 7

long 13

spotted 9

striped 11